ideals
NOSTALGIA

A crystal spring beneath a bridge,
Strawberries growing wild,
Building castles in the sand
Was heaven as a child.

Roaming through the woodland
With mysteries yet untold,
All are splendors of the past,
Now etched in purest gold.

Helen Rush Ehler

ISBN 0-8249-1053-2

Publisher, Patricia A. Pingry
Editor, Peggy Schaefer
Art Director, Patrick McRae
Production Manager, Jan Johnson
Permissions, Kathleen Gilbert
Typography, Karen Davidson

Front and back covers from H. Armstrong Roberts

Inside front cover by Ralph Luedtke

Inside back cover from Freelance Photographers Guild

IDEALS—Vol. 44, No. 5 August MCMLXXXVII IDEALS (ISSN 0019-137X) is published eight times a year,
February, March, May, June, August, September, November, December
by IDEALS PUBLISHING CORPORATION, Nelson Place at Elm Hill Pike, Nashville, Tenn. 37214-8000
Second class postage paid at Nashville, Tennessee, and additional mailing offices.
Copyright © MCMLXXXVII by IDEALS PUBLISHING CORPORATION.
POSTMASTER: Send address changes to Ideals, Post Office Box 148000, Nashville, Tenn. 37214-8000
All rights reserved. Title IDEALS registered U.S. Patent Office.
Published simultaneously in Canada.

SINGLE ISSUE—$3.50
ONE-YEAR SUBSCRIPTION—eight consecutive issues as published—$15.95
TWO-YEAR SUBSCRIPTION—sixteen consecutive issues as published—$27.95
Outside U.S.A., add $4.00 per subscription year for postage and handling.

The cover and entire contents of IDEALS are fully protected by copyright and must
not be reproduced in any manner whatsoever. Printed and bound in U.S.A.
by the Banta Co., Menasha, Wisconsin.

Come Walk with Me

Come walk with me
   Along the way where black-eyed
   Susans grow;
Come see the stately hollyhocks
   All blooming in a row.

Come look at velvet pansies
   With their funny little faces;
Come search the woods for wildflowers
   In their look-and-find-me places.

Come feel the petals of a rose,
   Like velvet to the touch;
Come pick the purple violets
   That children love so much.

Come walk with me
   And fill your eyes with all life's sweet
   surprises;
God's gift to us is flowers—
   All colors, shapes, and sizes.

Nelle Hardgrove

Photo Opposite
BLACK-EYED SUSANS
Michael Magnuson

Country Chronicle

Fifty years ago we harvested hay in the old way, with a mowing machine and a rake with large iron wheels. The modern mower, rake, and baler had not yet appeared in our part of the country. Haying was long and tiresome, extending from late June or early July well into August, the hottest days of the year. Yet these were also days of contentment and satisfaction. They took us to the fields, to the heartbeat of the land. I enjoyed riding behind the team of grays, and I loved the solace of the sun. There was music in the rhythmic clicking of knives on the cutting bar.

When the timothy cured, the rake, with its curving clanging tines, left long windrows across the meadow. Then with brawn and pitchfork, we transformed the windrows into haycocks and hauled them to the barn where

the hay was stored in the loft, under beams and rafters where swallows built.

I don't remember my age when my father decided it was time I learn the art of loading loose hay. Loading wasn't easy for a boy; binding it on the wagon to make it secure was difficult. Of all places, my father selected the steepest sidehill on the farm.

All went well, and when that first load was on the wagon, I started the team for the barn. Suddenly, the load slid off the rigging into a tangled, twisted mass on the downhill side. I dug myself free from the bulging mound and sheepishly climbed back on the wagon. I expected a stern reprimand as my father struggled to pull the hay apart and pitch it back on the wagon, but he never said a word. His silence was certainly out of character, and I

wonder now if he, too, might have met the same fate when he was loading his first hay, perhaps in that very same field.

I still occasionally spot an old mowing machine or a hay rake, rusting in tall weeds by an abandoned barn or shed, or by a stone wall overgrown with bushes and vines. Almost hidden from view, they bring back fond memories of the peace and serenity of August meadows speckled with haycocks at sundown.

I relish these summer days and the field sparrow's song. I walk the fields now just to enjoy the aroma of timothy and clover, the new-mown hay, the carrot-like scent of Queen Anne's lace, the rich sweet fragrance of the wild evening primrose, delighting in smells which remind me of those long but enjoyable haying seasons of my youth.

Lansing Christman

The Lake Isle of Innisfree

I will arise and go now, and go to Innisfree,
And a small cabin build there, of clay and wattles made:
Nine bean-rows will I have there, a hive for the honeybee,
And live alone in the bee-loud glade.

And I shall have some peace there, for peace comes dropping slow,
Dropping from the veils of the morning to where the cricket sings;
There midnight's all a glimmer, and noon a purple glow,
And evening full of the linnet's wings.

I will arise and go now, for always night and day
I hear lake water lapping with low sounds by the shore;
While I stand on the roadway, or on the pavements grey,
I hear it in the deep heart's core.

W. B. Yeats

AMERICAN CROSSROADS

Editor's Note: "American Crossroads" is a regular feature of *Ideals*, presenting photographs, stories, and jokes which have been submitted by our readers, about uniquely American events or experiences. If you have a 50 to 75 word account or photograph of an unusual or interesting occurrence unique to an American lifestyle or heritage, we would like to know. Send your submission to "American Crossroads," c/o Ideals Editorial, P.O. Box 141000, Nashville, TN 37214-1000. Please send only copies of manuscripts and duplicates of photographs or slides since submissions will not be returned. We will pay $10 for each printed submission.

Each year in the small town of Nevada, Iowa, citizens gather in celebration of "Lincoln Highway Days." This celebration is a tribute to the United States' first transcontinental automobile route. Officially known as the Lincoln Highway, in honor of our country's sixteenth president, the original route has changed considerably; however, roadmarkers and signs remain, a source of pride to the cities and towns through which the thoroughfare passed.

"Lincoln Highway Days" was begun in order to provide a look back at an important part of our country's heritage; and while the event was originally local in nature, participants now come from around the state and the nation. This year's celebration, which is to be held August 29th and 30th, will include a parade, a carnival, historical and collector exhibits, and entertainment.

Cecilia Landis
Nevada, Iowa

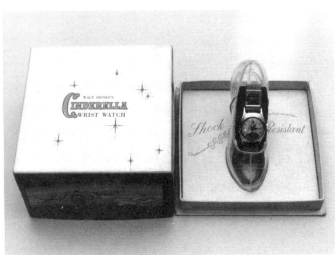

Howard Brenner, of Rochester, New York, has developed a hobby which literally takes him back "in time." He collects comic character clocks and watches.

Brenner's collection, which began with the purchase of a Roy Rogers alarm clock, has grown to nearly 150 timepieces. From Donald Duck to Superman, almost every popular childhood character is represented. Mickey Mouse, of course, is most prominent, as it was this character which started the comic watch phenomenon back in 1933. It is Brenner's 1934 Big Bad Wolf clock, however, which is one of his most prized possessions. Cunningly illustrated in red and black, the clock features the wolf on the left side of the face and the three little pigs cowering to the right.

Some watches carried patriotic or moral messages. For example, the back of the 1934 Tom Mix pocket watch is engraved: "Always find time for a good deed—Tom Mix." In addition, the novelty packaging of some comic character watches also made them attractive to parents and children. U.S. Time's 1954 Davy Crockett watch came wrapped around a plastic powder horn. And the 1950 Cinderella wristwatch actually came packaged in a replica of a glass slipper.

With watches such as these in his collection, it is not surprising that Howard Brenner's collection is the envy of the Disney Archives. After all, the majority of the comic timepieces feature Disney characters.

Ann McCutchan
Austin, Texas

Three Old-Fashioned Loves

In the years long ago, by an old country road,
There once stood an old-fashioned home
With a quaint, white-washed fence and a wee, swinging gate
And a chimney of field-gathered stone.
The sparkling-clean windows and old sagging door
Smiled a welcome to each passerby,
While in yon lovely garden, the hollyhocks swayed
In the breeze 'neath the blue summer sky.

An old-fashioned hearth decorated the room
Of that long-ago, old-fashioned home;
Oft 'round it we'd gather—family and friends.
By the firelight's glow, Dad would read the Good Book
While we children would gather around,
And Mother would rock in her old rocking chair,
Which creaked a melodious sound.

Just an old-fashioned home, an old-fashioned hearth,
An old-fashioned mother and dad;
Oh, but blessings as these, which I fondly recall,
Are the best that a child could have had.
And though changes are wrought by the fleeting years,
For these I will ever be glad—
An old-fashioned home, an old-fashioned hearth,
And an old-fashioned mother and dad.

Loise Pinkerton Fritz

Photo Opposite
MOUNTAIN SCENE
Larry Burton

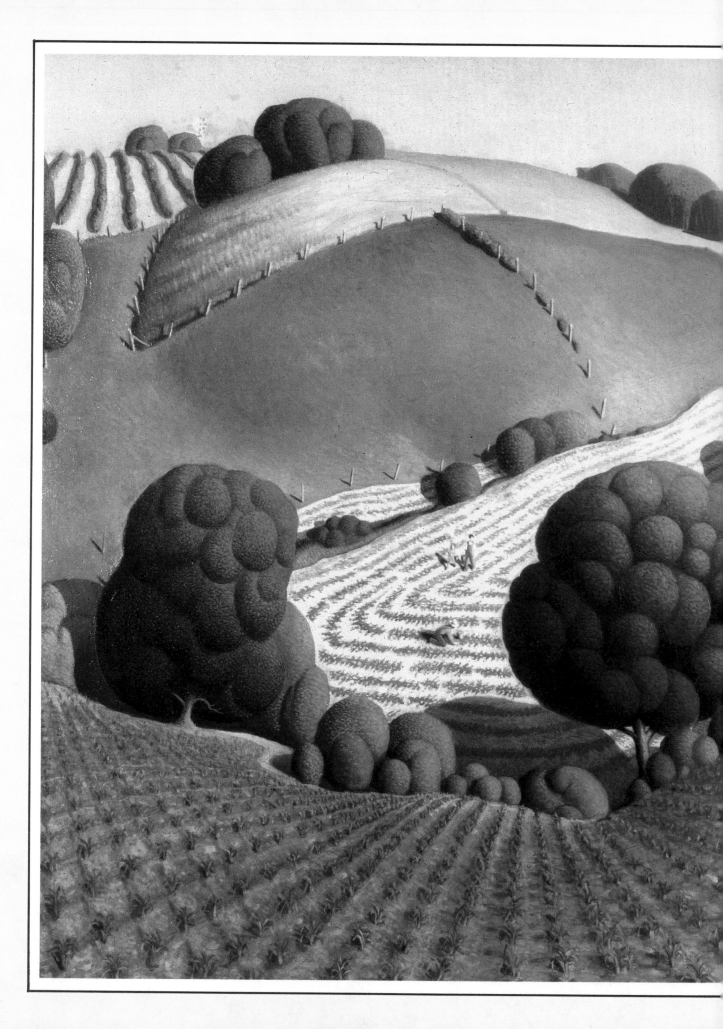

Grant Wood

1892 - 1942

Born in 1892, Grant Wood became one of the leading exponents of Midwestern Region-alism, a movement which dominated the American art scene in the 1930's. Believing artists should paint from personal experiences based on their local heritage, most of Wood's paintings portrayed the people and land-scapes of Iowa, where he was born and lived most of his life.

The realism and precise details in Wood's paintings show the influence of fifteenth and sixteenth century German and Flemish paint-ers. Simple geometric shapes and sharp con-tours dominate his compositions. Among Wood's better-known works are *Daughters of Revolution*, *Woman with Plants*, and *American Gothic*. Grant Wood died near his hometown of Anamosa, Iowa, in 1942.

YOUNG CORN
Grant Wood
Courtesy of The Cedar Rapids
Museum of Art,
Cedar Rapids Community
School District Collection, 1970

Readers'

Antique Doll

Standing straight
In the polished case,
Her dress of gingham
Trimmed in lace,

She seems to be
So lonely there,
Her blue eyes fixed
In dreamy stare.

Is she recalling
The long ago
And little girls
Who loved her so?

Mildred Dahlgren
Chicago, Illinois

When Life Was Simple

The good old days have disappeared,
    but memories still remain
Of a time when life was simple
    and most things stayed the same.

A nickel bought a lot of things—
    like candy bars and cones.
And families all went visiting,
    no need for telephones.

On Sunday we had company,
    served homemade lemonade;
Then sat upon the back porch steps—
    the oak tree gave us shade.

A good cigar cost just a dime,
    a movie ticket, too.
And "hand-me-downs" were welcome, 'cause
    they looked as good as new.

I had no worries as a child;
    that's why I can't forget
Those days were happy, even though
    there were no TV sets.

The one thing I am sure of—
    a great home life we shared!
We always knew that we were loved,
    and knew our parents cared.

Angie Monnens
Richmond, Minnesota

Reflections

Our Homemade Swing

A homemade swing hung in our yard
Between a tree and post;
And of my childhood memories,
'Tis one I think of most.

We climbed upon—both boys and girls—
The arms and back and seat;
The wonder is it didn't fall
And leave us in a heap!

No matter how we had to sit,
We'd never mind at all;
But we would swing and swing and sing
Until the night would fall.

The days of childhood come to mind
And many thoughts they bring—
Of love and laughter, girls and boys
And our old homemade swing.

Hazel Rugg
Corning, Ohio

Editor's Note: Readers are invited to submit unpublished, original poetry, short anecdotes, and humorous reflections on life for possible publication in future *Ideals* issues. Please send copies only; manuscripts will not be returned. Writers will receive $10 for each published submission. Send materials to ''Readers' Relfections,'' Ideals Publishing Corporation, Nelson Place at Elm Hill Pike, Nashville, Tennessee 37214.

Poppies

Poppies basking in the sun,
Aren't you lovely, every one!
Brilliant is your large bouquet
Spread across the hills today.

Waltzing in the summer breeze,
Flirting with the nodding trees,
Treasured beauty to behold—
Poppies...orange, red, and gold.

Petaled faces lifted up,
Catching sunbeams in each cup;
As the sun in skies serene
Casts its glow upon your scene.

God has touched the hills today
With your colorful display;
Poppies...orange, red, and gold—
A summer's dream my heart can hold.

Beverly J. Anderson
Ft. Lauderdale, Florida

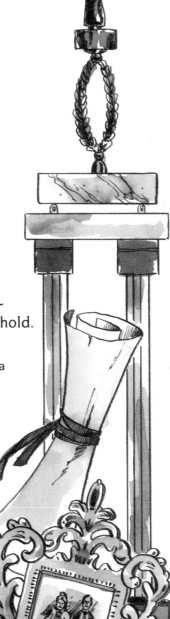

Streak of Gold

This afternoon a tiny yellow gleam
Of sunshine slithered through the cabin wall,
And burned again like fire across the small
Forsaken room, to wake my childhood dream.
So many years have passed, and yet they seem
So very few since Mother watched me crawl
About the floor in ecstacy, and call
For her to help me catch the rippling beam.

The little shack is weather worn and musty
(No busy hands are here to keep it now),
But when my heart is torn, I come to pray
And watch the streak of sun across the dusty
Cabin floor—a streak of gold—a vow
Of tender love returned from yesterday.

                                        Van Chandler

For John's Girl

It was with a heavy heart that I went to the college, a day or so before the opening, to withdraw and pack my mementos, books, and pictures. It seemed that I would never have the courage to leave. Once more I began to figure ways and means. There was no alternative, I concluded; it was clear that I would have to give up and say good-bye as quickly as possible.

I was on the verge of weeping, when I heard footsteps hurrying down the corridor. It was Jessie, the pretty, pink-cheeked maid who looked after us as though we were her own sisters. "This special delivery letter arrived for you last night," she said. "It looks important."

I tore it open nervously; it was from Griff Lewis, the Cripple Creek druggist and one of my father's good friends. Why under the sun was he sending me a letter by special delivery!

It had come back to Cripple Creek, he wrote, that I was going to give up college, and my father's friends were disturbed about it. Some of them had been wondering, he continued, if the sum of $150, to be sent at the rate of fifteen dollars a month, would help pull me through the year. The words danced before my eyes.

By evening I had calmed down enough to compose a dignified reply to Griff Lewis, accepting the generous offer, but only on the condition that it be regarded as a loan. This arrangement was agreed upon, and as the monthly post office orders began to arrive, I became aware of a growing sense of obligation.

A few days before Commencement, I received notification of my appointment to teach Spanish and history in the Victor High School. My salary would be $1,080 a year. The notification was signed by Griff Lewis, president of the School Board of the Cripple Creek District. It was the last place I wanted to go, and I read it through several times, hoping to dispel the shadow of gloom. I dreaded ever returning to the camp. It seemed as though I were fated to repeat the pattern of my mother's life.

Early in September, I went to Victor to begin my work as a teacher. After bills were paid, exactly seven dollars were left out of my first warrant; five were to go toward repaying the loan from Griff

Lewis. He had gone home for lunch when I arrived at the pharmacy and wouldn't return for an hour. It was an unusually bright October day and I decided to stroll out to Golden Avenue. I had not been there for more than two years, not since my mother's death in the faded yellow house on the corner.

The neighborhood had changed completely since we had lived there. The ungainly clapboard place my father had built after the fires appeared much smaller. Now it was empty and dilapidated; the windows were broken and glass littered the ground.

I sat for a while on the steps of the back porch, looking out over the camp. It was still a squalid, ugly town. Its only redeeming feature was in the kindliness of the human beings who had drifted there, by chance, in search of gold. "They're the salt of the earth," my father had often said. "A real Cripple Creeker stands by you to the end, and never forgets you when he makes his stake—no matter where he goes."

The three o'clock train started slithering around the shoulder of Bull Hill on its descent into camp. I got up quickly, remembering my business with Griff Lewis, and hurried down the creaky steps out of the yard.

I started to introduce myself as he held out his hand. "You don't have to tell me who you are," he said. "I'd almost know you in the dark—you look so much like John! Sit down," he said, pulling up a chair near his desk. "I want to hear how things are going."

I reassured him that all was well, but I felt strangely uncomfortable in spite of his warm friendly manner. "I'm very glad to meet you again after so many years," I began awkwardly. "I've heard my father speak of you often. He admired you very much. If he could know about all that you have done for me, he would be deeply grateful." My words sounded stilted, not as I had intended to say them. "I owe you a great debt—my position in the Victor High School as well as—"

"Now wait," he interrupted. "I'll grant that as president of the School Board my approval carries a little weight, but not enough to secure the appointment of an inferior or poorly equipped candidate."

"But there is something more—perhaps I should have mentioned it first," I replied, determined to go directly to the point. "I mean the loan that made it possible for me to finish college. I've come to arrange to repay you."

"Was it called a loan?" he asked after a moment. "I've forgotten, but I confess that no credit is due me for lending you the money; I was only the lucky go-between." He got up suddenly and went into a wide alcove and began to fumble among the empty medicine bottles on a shelf. At last he brought out a large glass fishbowl and set it on the desk in front of me. On one side, printed in golden letters, was the inscription, "For John's Girl."

I felt mystified and wondered what this had to do with me or the loan. Then he grinned like a young boy with an exciting secret. "First, I want to say something about your father; it'll help you to understand the rest better," he began, looking through me with his narrowed eyes. "Everybody who knew John, and that meant most of the men in camp, respected him. Oh, he had his weaknesses along with all of us. For one thing, he drank too much and gambled when it brought hardship to his family, but that isn't uncommon in a mining camp."

He reached for the fishbowl and polished the letters with his hand. "What you should always remember is that he had a consuming wish for you and never failed to speak of it to the friends who went to visit him. He told them that all he asked of the Almighty was to let him live long enough to know that you had finished your college education. 'If she turns out to be a fine woman,' he once said, 'fitted to stand up and look the world in the eye, then I guess she'll forgive my faults and my life won't have been for nothing.'

"The Bennett Avenue boys knew, of course, that John hadn't left a penny," Griff Lewis continued, "and that you'd have to give up school. Then a few of 'em came into my drugstore one night with a proposition. They wanted to finish the job for him and asked me how to go about it. Somebody suggested the idea of putting a fishbowl on my showcase where spare cash could be dropped now and then. I printed the gold letters on it and agreed to send you the money orders every month. That's all I had to do with it—I give you my word."

The truth had begun to dawn on me. "Then it really wasn't a loan from you?"

"Every cent came that way—from your father's friends," Griff Lewis nodded. "It beat all, the way the money rolled into that fishbowl! Poker win-

nings, lucky bets, overtime pay, extra dividends, unexpected royalties—even the purse for an impromptu prize fight at the Newport saloon. Nothing was too big or too small to put in the pot for John's girl.

"I'd like to thank every one of them," I said, struggling for self-control. "Could you tell me their names?"

"You've got me there," he said, smiling. "I couldn't tell you if my life depended on it. Fact is, I never knew 'em all—impossible to keep track of everybody coming to the store."

"But surely there must be somebody to...to..." I couldn't finish the sentence.

"Not one of 'em ever expected a word of thanks," Griff Lewis said, putting his hand on my arm. "They wanted to make your father's dream come true. What they did was for John's girl."

The four o'clock whistles had blown when I left the Lewis Pharmacy, and the sidewalk was crowded with miners just off dayshift. I scanned their faces eagerly, hoping to recognize some I had seen before who might have been among my father's friends. They were all strangers to me and oblivious to my gazing; and yet I felt an odd, tingling kinship with them. It seemed to me, as I hurried down Bennett Avenue, that I had come home, at last, to my father's world and had found warmth and human kindness beyond measure or understanding.

Mabel Barbee Lee

Circus Days

Circus days
  are coming soon;
Candied apples
  and ballons!
Clowns will wear
  their funny faces
And big shoes
  With fat shoelaces!

Lion trainers
  with their hoops,
Acrobats and
  loop-de-loops!
Popcorn, peanuts,
  Cracker jack
Will add pleasure
  to their acts!

Big top laughter,
  loud and clear,
Is the happy sound
  you'll hear.
Circus days are filled
  with fun,
For the old
  and for the young!

Kay Hoffman

Photo Opposite
CIRCUS WAGON
Laatsch-Hupp Photo

The Medicine Show

Many, many years ago,
As summer's heat would dance,
Impatiently we'd all await
The medicine show's advance.

The wagon would be painted
In colors bright and gay;
A span of handsome horses
Would lead the merry way.

Parading through our Main Street
Down to the vacant lot,
With calliope a-whistling,
Flags streaming from the top.

The hammering and sawing
To construct a small platform,
Where later in the evening
We'd see them all perform.

Of course there would be singing
Old songs like Clementine,
The simple routine of soft shoe;
Oh, it was really fine.

The magic-mulled elixir
Guaranteed, so we were told,
To cure all kinds of human ills
From corns to growing old.

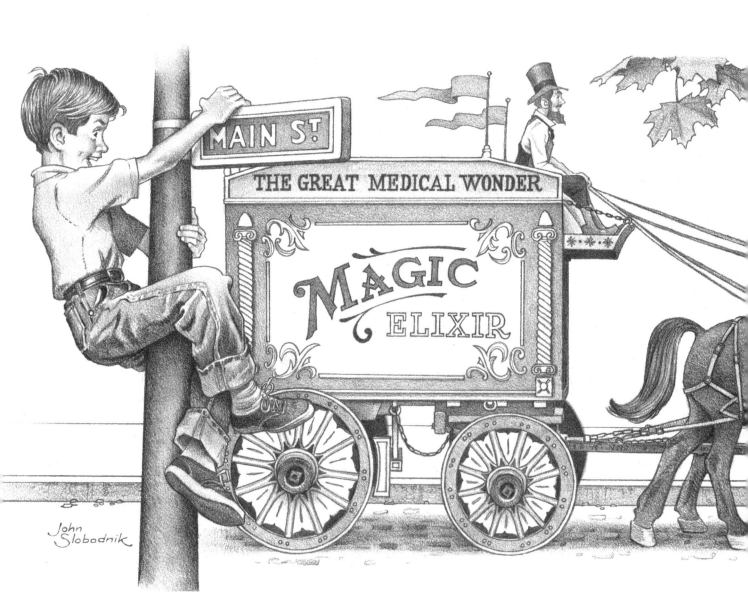

Wood-cutting contests followed,
Strictly for the ladies there;
We wished that we were old enough
And in the race could share.

At last our favorite moment,
For which we'd waited long,
The big full-blooded Indian Chief
Came thumping his tom-tom.

Fierce war whoops he'd be shouting,
Waving tomahawk in air;
We crouched in awe and wonder,
Shuddering in our chairs.

Too soon the fun was over;
We'd sigh in disbelief.
Our hearts were willing captives
Of that great Indian Chief.

One full week the show ran;
'Twas hard to wait each day.
When it finally finished up,
We waved it on its way.

The highlight of the summer
Had come to quickly pass,
Dejectedly we must now wait
Another year—alas.

Ethel H. Schnaars

The County Fair

On a wonderful day like today,
There's a glorious sun in the sky;
And a rainbow of colors is seen
Where banners are flying high,
While the cries of laughter and mirth
Ring out from the carousel
As we gaze at the jubilant crowd
And the sights too wondrous to tell!

There's enchantment wherever we go
Down the length of the gay midway,
Where pink cotton candy is spun
And popcorn is on display.
The barkers wait to entice us
To seek after a beautiful prize,
To reach for the blue of the heavens
On a thrilling, spinning ride.

There's beautiful red and blue ribbons
Where handiwork lines the halls...
The aprons, skirts, and dresses,
The wedding ring quilts and shawls.
While the crops from field and garden
Are arranged to please the eye,
The homemade cakes and cookies
Draw a lingering look and sigh.

There are champion roosters and hens
And thoroughbred horses and cows;
There are frolicking lambs and calves
That draw the admiring crowds.
There are whirligig birds and balloons
And sights too wondrous to tell,
But what makes today a wonderful day
Is our ride on the carousel!

Joy Belle Burgess

Days of Yore

I think the days of childhood
We all remember best;
They were the magic time of life
When every hour was blessed.

Each day was sort of special
With a joy of little things;
Our hearts were full of laughter
And our feet had golden wings.

School days kept us busy;
But when the bell tolled three,
Through every passing season
There were things to do and see.

Holidays were wonderful;
Vacation time was grand.
The whole world seemed to nestle
Within our tiny hand.

Our pennies went for soda pop,
Ice cream and candy, too;
We'd share it with our chums and pets,
The way good fellows do.

The realm of sleep was peaceful,
Not a trouble or a care;
We saw happiness and beauty
Around us everywhere.

LaVerne P. Larson

Mama's Pie

I was nine the summer Mama taught me how to bake a pie. It was an occasion, a rite of passage, a journey back into family history. The lesson was full of truth, pungent as our wild berries, liberally dusted with flour, and punctuated with the wooden rolling pin.

I stood next to the cutting board, my dress covered with a folded dishtowel, cinched around my middle and tied at the back.

"You take this much flour," Mama said, dumping an undisclosed amount in a large bowl, "then you add shortening—about this much." She dropped a glob of the sticky white stuff into the flour. "Now a pinch of salt. Take this pastry cutter and cut through the flour and shortening until it looks like cornmeal. Here now, you do it."

I had no idea what cornmeal looked like, but I kept cutting through the mixture, certain Mama would give me a hint when it got to the right stage. After a bit, the flour and shortening were crumbly and coarse. Mama looked at it, nodded, and announced it was time to add the water.

"You never dump water into pie dough," Mama warned. "You sprinkle it on, a tiny bit at a time. Use your hand like this."

She dipped her fingers into a cup of water and shook the drops over the mixture, tossing it now and then with a fork. When the dough could be pressed together into a crumbly ball, she stopped, took about half of the mixture out of the bowl, and pressed it together into an oval on the floured board.

"Now you roll it out," she said, "but only roll it once. Pie crust is like people—you treat them gently and they turn out tender, but if you keep pushing and pressing them, they'll turn out tough and tasteless every time."

I rolled—center to edge—all around the circle.

"Don't worry if it crumbles around the edges," Mama said, noting my frustration. "That's the best sign of a good batch!" Gently we transferred the flattened dough into the pie plate.

"Now the berries." The tart wild black- berries, frosted with sugar and flour and seeping with purple juice, tumbled into the waiting pie shell. We had picked them the day before, hunting through the burned-off growth in the woods behind the cemetery. I still bore scars from the adventure: hairline scratches laced my hands and purple stains outlined my fingernails. These berries were earned with sweat and blood and would taste all the better for our efforts.

After I rolled the top crust, Mama cut a curved line across its center. "Just like my Mama used to do," she murmured. She crimped the edges with her finger and thumb, deftly creating a scalloped border around the pie. After brushing the top crust with cream, we slipped the pie into the oven, and Mama put on the teakettle—a sign we were to have a talk.

When the china cups were filled and steaming, Mama pulled two chairs up to the table and we sat. For the first time, I sensed that Mama and I were somehow equals and I felt special, privy to some feminine world I'd never known before. Mama stirred her tea and started to talk, introducing me to her past, the time before she was Mama.

"We were poor kids," she said, "but we never knew it. Daddy and Mama raised ten of us on a small farm where we had a little garden, a pasture, and an orchard, all sur- rounded by woods. We always had fresh or canned vegetables, milk from the cow, and plenty of eggs, even during the depression. And Mama always made pies. There were green apple pies and pumpkin pies, even mince meat when one of the neighbors had good luck hunting and got a deer. But the favorite was always wild blackberry pie. We kids called them 'little creepy crawlers' because in the woods behind our house, the vines crept along the forest floor, tangling themselves around stumps and over stones. We'd clamber through the prickly vines, searching for the sweet, dark berries and plopping them into our tin lard buckets. The smell of the berries, warm from the sun, was heavenly; and we ate as many as we saved, staining our fingers and lips with the purple juice.

"My mother baked the pies as soon as we returned with the fruit. She always hummed while she baked, flour dust rising about her like a cloud and settling on her hair and faded cotton dress."

"Is that when you learned how to bake pies, Mama?" I asked, trying to imagine my mother as a young girl, scratched and stained with berry juice and filled with the same insecurities and sense of wonder as I.

"Yes," Mama said and her lips curved in a smile, soft with remembrance. "I was just about your age, and I remember I had to stand on an apple crate to reach the counter top."

The fragrance of the baking pie wound around us, casting a spell of homey intimacy as we sipped our tea, sharing our heritage until the timer interrupted us with a rude buzz. As we removed the steaming pie from the oven, Mama sighed with satisfaction and said, "There, now that's a job well done." And somehow I know she meant more than just the baking of the pie.

The summer afternoon of my first pie was more than thirty years ago, and yet its memories are as sweet and real as the berries in the bowl before me. I think it's time to call my daughter in from play and show her how to bake a pie. Perhaps we'll sit and share a cup of tea while it bakes, and I will tell her how her great-grandma used to bake a pie.

Pamela Kennedy

Mama's Wild Blackberry Pie

4 cups wild blackberries
1 cup sugar
3 tablespoons flour
2 cups flour
⅔ cup shortening
pinch of salt
¼ to ⅓ cup cold water

Toss berries, sugar, and flour together lightly in a large bowl and set aside.

Place flour, shortening, and salt in a bowl. Combine ingredients using a pastry blender until mixture is coarse and crumbly and texture is uniform.

Sprinkle water over mixture, 1 tablespoon at a time, tossing with a fork after each addition. Add only enough water to hold dough together— don't add too much water!

Form ⅔ of dough into a ball. Roll out dough on floured pastry cloth to ⅛-inch thickness using short, firm strokes of the rolling pin as you move around the circle from center to edge. Lift gently into 9-inch pie pan and trim off excess dough.

Pour prepared berries, sugar, and flour into pie shell.

Roll remaining dough and trimmings from bottom crust into circle for top crust. Cut curved design into top for steam vents. Trim excess dough and crimp edges together with finger and thumb. Brush top with cream.

Bake at 425° for 30 minutes, then reduce heat to 350° for 30 minutes. Cool on rack. Pie may bubble over during second half hour, so you might want to place foil on oven bottom to catch drips.

Fern Hill

Now as I was young and easy under the apple
    boughs
About the lilting house and happy as the grass was
    green,
     The night above the dingle starry,
       Time let me hail and climb
     Golden in the heydays of his eyes,
And honoured among wagons I was prince of the
    apple towns
And once below a time I lordly had the trees and
    leaves
       Trail with daisies and barley
     Down the rivers of the windfall light.

And as I was green and carefree, famous among the
    barns
About the happy yard and singing as the farm was
    home,
     In the sun that is young once only,
       Time let me play and be
     Golden in the mercy of his means,
And green and golden I was huntsman and herds-
    man, the calves
Sang to my horn, the foxes on the hills barked clear
    and cold,
       And the sabbath rang slowly
     In the pebbles of the holy streams.

All the sun long it was running, it was lovely, the
    hay
Fields high as the house, the tunes from the
    chimneys, it was air
     And playing, lovely and watery
       And fire green as grass.
       And nightly under the simple stars
As I rode to sleep the owls were bearing the farm
    away,
All the moon long I heard, blessed among stables,
    the nightjars
       Flying with the ricks, and the horses
       Flashing into the dark.

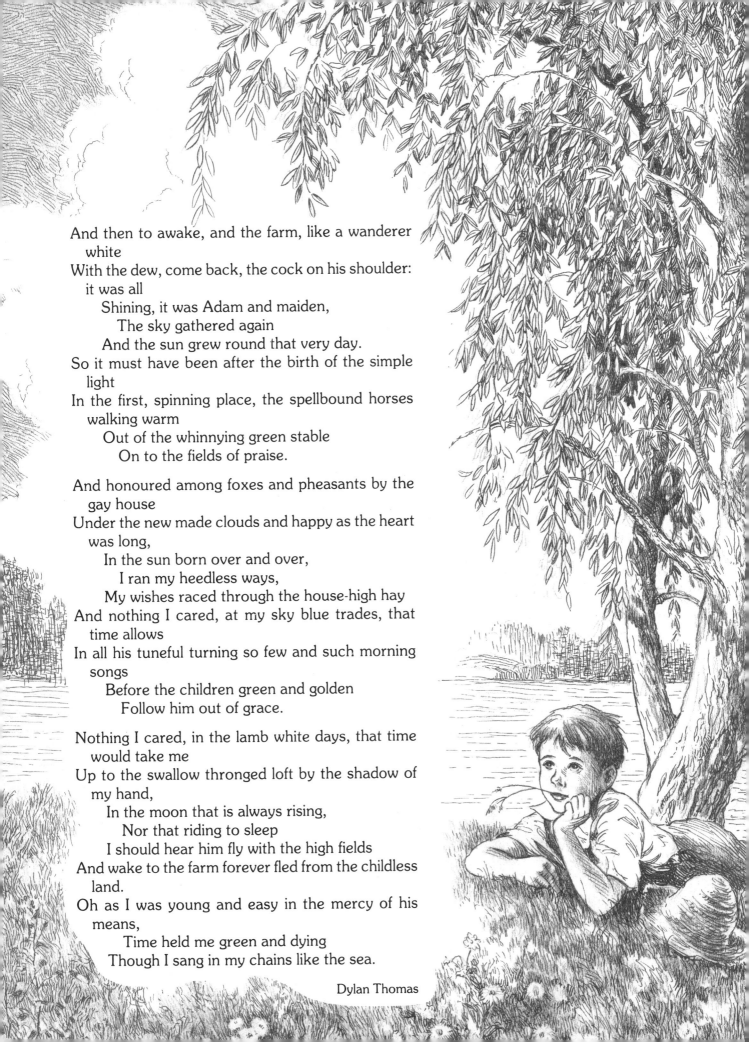

And then to awake, and the farm, like a wanderer white
With the dew, come back, the cock on his shoulder: it was all
    Shining, it was Adam and maiden,
      The sky gathered again
    And the sun grew round that very day.
So it must have been after the birth of the simple light
In the first, spinning place, the spellbound horses walking warm
    Out of the whinnying green stable
      On to the fields of praise.

And honoured among foxes and pheasants by the gay house
Under the new made clouds and happy as the heart was long,
    In the sun born over and over,
      I ran my heedless ways,
    My wishes raced through the house-high hay
And nothing I cared, at my sky blue trades, that time allows
In all his tuneful turning so few and such morning songs
    Before the children green and golden
      Follow him out of grace.

Nothing I cared, in the lamb white days, that time would take me
Up to the swallow thronged loft by the shadow of my hand,
    In the moon that is always rising,
      Nor that riding to sleep
    I should hear him fly with the high fields
And wake to the farm forever fled from the childless land.
Oh as I was young and easy in the mercy of his means,
    Time held me green and dying
    Though I sang in my chains like the sea.

Dylan Thomas

When Dreams Cost a Nickel

A coin was a treasure
To hold and adore,
When dreams cost a nickel
And I was just four.

I plotted and planned
And nursed visions galore
Of treats I would buy
At the old candy store.

The barrels of anise,
The licorice sticks,
The salt water taffies
Were all up for licks.

With wealth in my hand,
I would run to the store,
When dreams cost a nickel
And I was just four.

Craig E. Sathoff

CABOT'S CANDY
SALT WATER
TAFFY
MADE RIGHT HERE
Natural
ICE CREAM

Hometown Band

There was nothing quite as lively
As our little hometown band;
The conductor raised his arms up
    high
With his baton in hand.

The jolly little trumpet man
Blew his golden horn,
Forceful was the strain he played
Like a rooster crowing in morn.

The soothing melodious clarinets
Lilted along with glee,
Making the audience want to dance
To their magical melody.

The thumpety thump of the big
    bass drum
Made you tap your foot so free.
Yes, the melodies of our hometown
    band
Hold many a memory for me.

Ruth H. Underhill

The Bandstand

The bandstand held the spotlight
In the village park each year.
And the music that the band played
Reached out both far and near.

The crowd sat upon benches
Placed where all could clearly hear
Refrains which were a pleasure
And a treat to every ear.

The children took advantage
Of the concert as a cue
To play friendly rounds of tag,
Or another game or two.

Band leaders seemed elated
When the members played so well,
And evenings were relaxing
As the music cast a spell.

So summers in the village,
When nights were hot and long,
Were greatly enchanted when
The bandstand burst with song.

Mildred Potts

Remember When...

adventure, romance, mystery, drama, and music were only as far away as the nearest radio—whether it be the cathedral-like Atwater Kent on the library table or the massive Stromberg Carlson console in the corner of the living room. Throughout the 1930's and 1940's radio was the king of entertainment.

We laughed at the antics of Charlie McCarthy and Edgar Bergen, Fred Allen, Jack Benny, and a host of other comedians; sat spellbound as the Shadow asked, "Who knows what evil lurks in the hearts of men?"; followed faithfully the adventures of Helen Trent (romance can live in life at thirty-five and after), Ma Perkins, Mary Noble, and *One Man's Family;* and enjoyed the fine drama of the *Lux Radio Theater* and the *Mercury Theater of the Air.* We spent Sunday afternoons listening to the broadcasts of the New York Philharmonic Symphony and the Metropolitan Opera. There were musical variety shows—Kay Kyser's *College of Musical Knowledge,* Rudy Vallee and the *Fleischmann Hour,* and that weekly favorite, *Your Hit Parade.*

Kate Smith, *Major Bowes' Amateur Hour,* the *Kraft Music Hall,* Mr. Keen, *Easy Aces, Voice of Firestone,* Robert Trout, Edward R. Murrow, H. V. Kaltenborn, all of these are part of a marvelous era when radio brought laughs, thrills, excitement, tears and happiness into our lives. Every now and then, a forgotten tune, the appearance of an old friend on television, or perhaps the sight of a dust-covered, magical box tucked away in an attic corner reminds us of those wonderful years when radio was monarch and we were its enchanted, loyal, and adoring subjects.

Barely a Lifetime

The First World War was rapidly becoming a dim memory; only a few visionaries dreamed that a second one was only a few years off.

America was still trying to shake off the grip of the Great Depression, an era in American history that most would agree was not really so "great." For most people, life was still hard, a daily struggle to survive.

Millions turned to Hollywood for laughs, for tears, for joy, for excitement. And Hollywood paid off handsomely. Going to the movies was one of the few great investments of the time: for perhaps a nickel, certainly no more than a dime, one could have hours of pleasure at places with names like "Rialto," "Palace," "Strand," "Knickerbocker," "Paramount," "Princess," and "Rex." It seemed as if every town in America had at least one movie house.

Who can forget the hot, summer, Saturday afternoons when we escaped to the movies? Chores were finished quickly and neatly to get to the theatre. Quarter in hand, we stood before the glass cage and gained admission to the sanctuary. Inside, the toasty, buttery, popcorn popping delighted our ears and sparkled our sense of smell. We loaded up with boxes of popcorn, cold drinks, and the most wonderful candy bars in the world—that sold for only a nickel.

In the cool darkness, we watched, enchanted, as Roy Rogers and Gene Autry tamed the west. Hepburn and Tracy taught us about love; William Powell and Myrna Loy taught us wit and style. Vivien Leigh and Clark Gable held us spellbound as a world of grace and gentility was swept up in *Gone With The Wind.*

Laurel & Hardy and the Marx Brothers doubled us over with laughter. Buck Rogers kept us on the edge of our seats as he battled evil in the 21st century. We booed Edward G. Robinson as the bad guy.

The cartoon, the newsreel, and the endless previews of coming attractions were almost as much a thrill as the movie we eagerly awaited. Popcorn never tasted so good, nor soda as sweet and tingly, as it did when we were settled back in the plush, crushed velvet of a movie theatre seat.

There were so many great screen stars of the thirties. And there were so many "character actors," whose names we didn't know but whose faces we recognized over and over again, from one movie to the next.

It's hard to believe it was only fifty or so years ago. Barely a lifetime. They brought us so much joy and pleasure and excitement. Many of our fondest memories are of sitting wide-eyed before the flickering images. For many of us, the movie stars we grew up with are as much a part of our youth and past as the neighbors next door.

So many of the great ones are gone. The few still remaining aren't making movies like they used to. But they live on, in our hearts and in our memories, and in the celluloid images that still show up on television late at night—the ones we still watch longingly, and lovingly.

Steven Womack

ADOLPH ZUKOR presents
CLARK GABLE
NO MAN
OF HER OWN
with
CAROLE LOMBARD
DOROTHY MACKAILL
DIRECTED BY WESLEY RUGGLES
A Paramount Picture

The Big Band

"The Big Band Era," some folks say,
As if those days are past;
But others know the big band sound
Will not be gone that fast.

The big band groups are fewer now,
But many still abound
To lend their beat, their muted horns,
Their harmony of sound.

JIMMY DORSEY AND HIS BAND
The Bettmann Archive

The big band sound has registered
A heritage of names:
Duke Ellington and Artie Shaw,
Glenn Miller, Harry James.

There's Whiteman, Dorsey, and Hampton,
There's Guy Lombardo, too,
And Goodman, Krupa, Henderson;
And this just names a few.

In fact, I think we treasure more
With every passing year
The big band sound and fellowship
Of people it draws near.

Craig E. Sathoff

The Old-Fashioned Car

An old-fashioned car is a handsome thing,
And a parade of such beauties will always bring
So many sweet memories quickly to view,
Memories of yesterday and happy times, too.

I'll never forget the old-fashioned car,
Nor the roaring and rattling or head-bouncing jars
When the skinny-wheeled "lizzie" hit the big ruts
Of an old country lane full of rocks and deep cuts.

And I'll never forget the fun of a ride
When rain whipped the isinglass curtains aside,
And water came splashing all over our faces
And the windshield was nothing but rivery laces.

At times the old car would get balky and stall;
There was no automatic starter at all.
But with some turns of a crank, the car roared with a jolt;
It vibrated and screeched at each connection and bolt.

Then the driver adjusted the gas and the gears
And took off with a racket that deafened our ears.
We laughed and we sang, the car's noise complying,
At a twenty-mile speed, we thought we were flying!

We made Sunday visits to the folks here and there
And went on some picnics and to the big county fair.
We followed the trails that were old wagon traces
And rode with the wind pushing hard on our faces.

Yes, the old-fashioned car was an exquisite thing,
And it made the proud owner feel like a rich king
As he sat stiff and straight, the steering wheel gripped tight.
He hung onto that wheel with all of his might!

The seats had coil springs; how we bounced on the bumps
When the car dropped in holes or ascended the humps.
Traveling by car in the old-fashioned days
Was rough and uncomfortable in a few dozen ways.

And it was with good reason; those old roads were rough.
But the old car could take it; it was built good and tough.
Those cars proved their worth in many harsh ways,
And they stir up fond memories of the long-ago days.

Helen Shick

America's Home Front

Although it was members of the United States armed forces who did the fighting and the dying in World War II, America's home front worked miracles toward the final victory. It was that white flame of total war that truly fused this whole nation together.

In the final analysis, it was the unique and massive financing (by the American taxpayer), huge production of armaments, and the ability to move this equipment abroad with dispatch that finally overpowered the Axis. For America was still the land of muscle (which the enemy mistakenly thought had become flabby) and it was good old American know-how that helped turn the tide. In 1939, two percent of our gross national product was armaments. By 1942, it quadrupled; by 1944 the United States assembly lines were generating fifty percent more war materials than the *total* enemy output. Private industry was converted overnight. Vacuum cleaner plants were making machine guns, cars turned into tanks and plane engines.

By 1944, three and one-half million "Rosie, the Riveters" stood side-by-side with six million men, turning out everything from cargo ships and planes at record speeds.

United States citizens bought forty-nine billion dollars in War Bonds. We grew our own food in Victory Gardens—large or small—even though the United States farmers were producing enough food to feed half a world and their armies.

Civil Defense Corps volunteers were bumping into each other spotting for planes and ships that were thousands of miles away.

Kids saved empty toothpaste tubes and all true-blue Americans turned into attic and basement scavengers, collecting any and all used metal. There were stockpiles of everything from old pots and pans to flattened-out tin cans.

Do you remember (perhaps even have one or two stowed away as souvenirs) your ration books? You were issued so many stamps in various colors for gasoline, cigarettes, meat, food—almost everything you wanted. Yet ironically, Americans ate *more* food and spent more money on it than at any other time previously.

From no longer available import sources

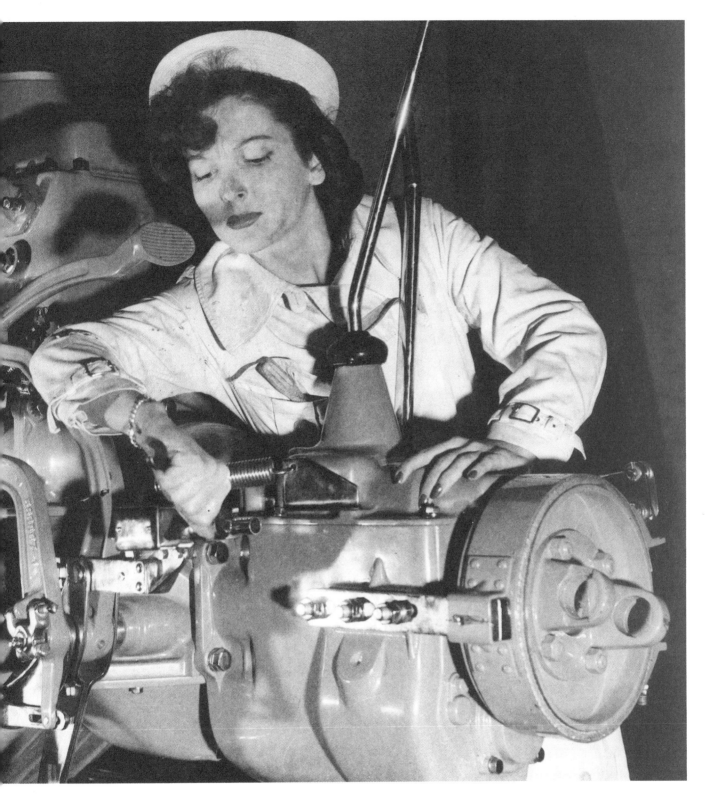

came new scientific discoveries for war. Radar was discovered and improved; flame throwers, rocket launchers, jet engines, and many other lethal weapons of war came into being.

And—for the betterment of man—penicillin and its successive antibiotics were discovered to cure what had been incurable diseases; DDT, to fight jungle insects, came home after the war; the use of blood plasma instead of whole blood has given life to multitudes.

Above all else, we rediscovered what Americans have always known: that when we come together for the *common* good with one common purpose, we have the will and the skill to win!

Old Things
Are More Beautiful

Old things are more beautiful
    than many things brand new
Because they bring fond mem'ries
    of things we used to do.

Old photographs in albums,
    love letters tied with lace,
Recapture those old feelings
    that new ones can't replace.

Baby shoes, a teddy bear,
    a ring that grandma wore,
Are treasures waiting there behind
    a door marked "Nevermore."

Old things are more beautiful,
    more precious day by day,
Because they are the flowers
    we planted yesterday.

Clay Harrison

Old Things

I love old things...old books, old friends,
　　The lovely way an old tree bends
Above a little clapboard house,
　　A tiny yard still as a mouse.

A zig-zag fence of cedar rails,
　　A stout old ship with mended sails,
Tall trees around a village square,
　　A chest of thin old silverware.

An old log house beyond the town,
　　Its oaken rafters falling down,
Yet holding in each chimney stone
　　An ageless beauty of its own.

I love the sheen of oaken floors,
　　Wrought-iron hinges on old doors,
The sound that flowing water makes,
　　The weathered brown of cedar shakes.

I love old things...timeworn and frayed,
　　Upon whose heart the years have laid
A kindly touch as if to show
　　The beauty of their inner glow.

Edna Jaques

Depression Glass

When times were hard and money scarce
    Many long years ago,
There was a tinted glassware
    That the housewives came to know.

In hues of pink and sometimes green,
    Its price not in excess,
It brought to many struggling homes
    Its humble loveliness.

When times improved and money came,
    This glass was put away
In attics, trunks, and cupboards high,
    While new glass held its sway.

In hues of pink and sometimes green,
    It bowed in humbleness,
While newer glasswares much in vogue
    Came forth in radiance.

But now that many years have passed,
    We welcome back once more
The beauty of depression glass
    To treasure and adore.

From attics, trunks, and cupboards high,
    In hues of pink or green,
We have returned its loveliness
    To reign with grace serene.

                    Craig E. Sathoff

Old Lamps

The lovely tiffany-type lamps
With shades of colored glass
In panels leaded side by side
Have faded to the past.

A few remain to grace our homes,
And they still proudly stand;
Their bases formed of metal
With sculpturing by hand.

The light they shed is mellow light,
And thoughts they call to mind
Are gentle thoughts of cozy times
And peace for all mankind.

So regal are the graceful shades
Which like umbrellas fall
That all the room seems filled with warmth,
And splendor reigns for all.

Craig E. Sathoff

Photo Opposite
TIFFANY WINDOW
Courtesy of
The Metropolitan Museum of Art
Anonymous Gift, 1981

The Quilting Bee

Their hearts were all in rhythm
With their fingers and their stitching
As they sewed the small straight stitches
That made Grandma's quilts bewitching.
They chatted and they tittered
As they lunched on cake and tea—
The sweet old-fashioned ladies
At the hometown quilting bee.

Prim in fresh-starched cotton
As they labored in a row
On quilts of intricate design
With pieces set "just so."
Their skillful fingers wove a spell
Of stitches laid with care,
To make a masterpiece to show
At many a county fair.

"Friendship" quilts and "Wedding Rings,"
Just to name a few;
Sunburst patterns, bright and gay,
Old-fashioned "Nine-patch," too;
"Rainbow" quilts and "Flower Pots"
In hand-sewn applique—
They never dreamed of machine-made quilts
Back in Grandma's day.

So here's to lovely ladies
And the fine heirlooms they made
While exchanging bits of gossip
At the local Ladies' Aid.
The art they plied was priceless
With their stitches, one-two-three—
The dedicated ladies
At the hometown quilting bee.

Nadine Brothers Lybarger

Old-Time Clambake

Sourdough Bread

Makes 2 loaves

1 package active dry yeast
1 cup boiling water
2 tablespoons sugar
2 tablespoons butter at
    room temperature
1½ cups Sourdough Starter
½ teaspoon salt
1 teaspoon white vinegar
4½ cups flour
1 tablespoon cornmeal
1 egg white

Combine yeast with ¼ cup warm water (105° to 115°) in a small glass bowl. Stir; set aside for 5 minutes in a draft-free area. Combine boiling water with sugar and butter in a separate bowl. Cool mixture until warm; add yeast mixture, sourdough starter, and salt. Add vinegar and 2 cups flour; mix together for 2 minutes or until the ingredients begin to form a dough. Work remaining flour into dough by kneading on a lightly floured board for 5 to 8 minutes or until dough is smooth. Place dough in a large greased bowl; turn dough once. Cover loosely; let rise for 1½ hours in a draft-free area or until doubled in bulk. Punch dough down; divide dough in half and place on lightly floured board. Form into two log shapes. Place loaves in greased bread pans sprinkled with cornmeal. Cover bread lightly; set aside for 1¼ hours or until doubled in bulk. Preheat oven to 400°. Cut slashes diagonally in loaves. Combine egg white with 2 tablespoons warm water; brush tops of bread with mixture. Bake for 35 minutes or until browned. Cool on rack before removing from pan.

Sourdough Starter

Makes 2 cups starter

1 package active dry yeast
2 cups flour
2 cups warm water

Combine yeast, flour, and 2 cups warm water (105° to 115°) in a glass bowl. Cover bowl; set aside at room temperature for 48 hours. Stir mixture twice each day. The starter will be bubbling. Refrigerate mixture after 48 hours. Stir mixture well before using. Ladle out amount required in recipe. Replenish the remaining starter each time by mixing in 1 cup flour and 1 cup warm water. Let starter stand uncovered in a warm area for 4 hours or until it begins to bubble. Cover loosely and refrigerate. Use and replenish within two weeks for continuing yeast action.

Backyard Clambake

Makes 6 servings

1 bushel seaweed, washed, still wet
6 live lobsters (1 pound each)
6 ears corn in the husk
3 pounds clams
 Melted butter

Use an outdoor fireplace or open barbecue pit for convenience. In the bottom of a very large, heavy kettle, place a layer of wet seaweed. Kill lobsters by severing vein at the base of the neck; arrange them over the seaweed. Add another layer of seaweed; top with corn in the husk. Add a third layer of seaweed; top with clams and a final layer of seaweed. Cover tightly and cook over hot fire for 2 hours or until clams are cooked. Discard any unopened clams. Serve clams first, then corn; serve the cooked lobster last. Serve with melted butter.

Keepsakes

Some building blocks, a teddy bear,
A china doll with painted hair,
A penny bank, a horse on wheels,
And little shoes with worn-down heels.

These keepsakes could such tales relate—
Old pewter mug, ABC plate,
Quaint paper dolls, white bunny, too,
And crooked pictures some child drew.

We keep them in a special place—
Nicked china cup and bits of lace,
Toy soldiers, and a watch whose face
Has no hands, shows toothmark's trace!

Old timeworn things are treasured now;
We cannot throw them out somehow,
Because about them memory twines
Its green and everlasting vines.

Ruth B. Field

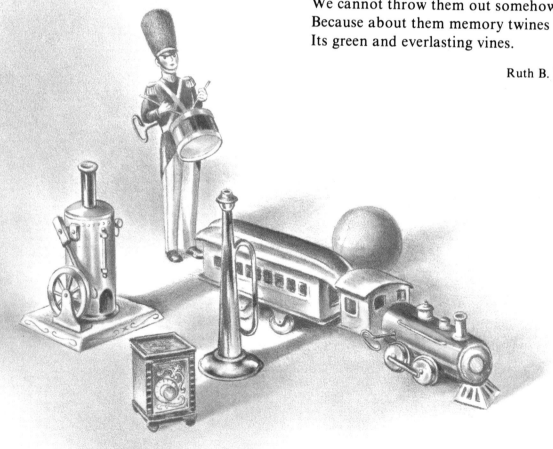

I'm going to throw out junk today...
Clean out the attic straight away.
Now is the time to start anew,
Off with the old...on with the new.

And so I started with a trunk
That I assumed was full of junk;
Out came a doll, so old, yet fair—
A dozen mem'ries lingered there;

A sampler that I painfully made
When I was in the second grade.
Some music books whose magic tunes
Stirred sweet romance in other Junes.

Love letters tied with bow of blue,
I read each over through and through.
An ivory fan, a faded rose,
How could I e'er try to dispose

Of such dear keepsakes, treasures all,
That so many mem'ries do recall.
I put them all back in the trunk;
These are my mem'ries...they're not junk!

Carice Williams

Doors of Memory

One night he needed something
Inside the cedar chest,
Some basketball equipment
That he had long possessed.

So there within the closet,
We searched, my son and I,
And laughed at some reminders
Of childhood passing by.

And then among the relics
Appeared a little toy,
A shiny metal toy train
He cherished as a boy.

It's strange how we can open
The doors of memory
And suddenly discover
The days that used to be.

Hilda Butler Farr

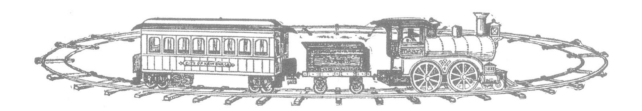

Cherished Treasure

We found her in the auction box
Bought at a sale last fall,
The contents, books and linens
And a lacy, silken shawl.

Underneath a cardboard cover,
To our complete surprise,
We found a doll of yesteryear
With brown curls and bright blue eyes.

Well wrapped in old newspaper,
Layered creases, yellow-white,
Tied up in faded ribbons
In small bows, once sunshine-bright.

Her dress was hand-stitched taffeta,
Trimmed in ruffled, ivory lace.
Her bonnet of blue velvet
Framed the dainty, porcelain face.

We wondered just how old she was
And what her name should be,
Then, looking at the crinkled skirt,
We solved one mystery.

In lettered fine embroidery,
Small stitches barely there,
Jenny Lee, her name was shown,
Firm letters clear and rare.

How many children played with her
And curled her long, brown hair?
How many in a hundred years
Have rocked her in their chair?

Which children held here tenderly,
Have owned and loved her well?
Jenny Lee sits in her rocking chair
And smiles, but will not tell.

Elisabeth Weaver Winstead

The Country School

I never see a modern school
With windows bright upon the street,
The latest books, the latest rule
To make each childish day complete,
But what I find the winding way
Through halls of memory again,
To where it's standing, shabby, gray—
The little schoolhouse in the lane!

Its windows, with their tiny panes,
Looked out upon the fields of wheat.
Its roof was stained with many rains;
Its steps were worn by shoeless feet.
My mother learned to read and spell
In that one schoolroom, quaint and plain.
Perhaps that's why I love so well
The little schoolhouse in the lane!

The water pail, the dipper, too,
The lunches high upon the shelf;
The warmth and comfort that we knew
Beside the stove I filled myself!
The country school of long ago
I'll not forget through years that wane.
It taught me all the good I know—
The little schoolhouse in the lane!

Anne Campbell

Photo Opposite
SCHOOLHOUSE INTERIOR
Rural Life Museum,
Louisiana State University
Alan Pitcairn
Grant Heilman Photography

The Singing Katydids

When nightfall cloaks the village
And darkness hides the hills,
When lights glow in the windows
And the air is summer filled,
Then wrapped in tiny breezes
That waft by, bit by bit,
Is the sweet and lovely night song
Of the singing katydids.

They render such a cheery tune,
And yet it's plaintive, too;
For I drift back in memory
When time was, oh, so new.
In family style we'd oftimes sit
Upon the big back porch
And listen to the katydids
When daytime chores were o'er.

When nightfall hides the village
And darkness cloaks the hills,
When all is calm and quiet
Down at the old grist mill,
'Tis then I hear the chorus
Of singing katydids...
On nature's music chart, it's still
One of the top-ten hits.

Loise Pinkerton Fritz

The Old Mill

A hundred years the mill has stood,
All huddled by this brook,
Until its gray and weathered shape
Bears now a rooted look!

The corn chaff and the brown wheat bran
Smell like aged musk,
And little mice with button eyes
Creep out to eat at dusk.

The candleglow and lantern light
Have cast vast shadows here,
As ancient millers lived their lives
Within this shaking sphere!

The seasons pass in slow parade,
The owners come and go;
The water turns the grinding wheel
In springtime or in snow.

The twilight softens every board
And lends enchanting grace,
For time itself has caravaned
In this nostalgic place.

Dorothy Evelyn Begg

Photo Opposite
DAYS OF YESTERDAY
Ken Dequaine

Summer
Memories

As summertime draws to a close
I sit and reminisce,
Remembering the joy it brought,
The hours filled with bliss.

How anxiously I waited for
Each warm and sunny day
To bring forth all its wonders
In a lovely, magic way.

My heart was quite enchanted
By the beauty everywhere;
The hills and fields were fairylands,
Sweet and green and fair.

The azure sky, the fluffy clouds,
Each flower bright and gay,
Were gifts I fondly treasure
In my memory today.

The seashore, too, held wondrous charm
Where water kissed the sands;
'Twas there I'd launch my ship of dreams
To far off mystic lands.

And fireflies of evening,
Like tiny lamps of gold,
Winging through the starry night
Were delightful to behold.

Though summertime is ending,
It will never quite depart,
Because its precious scenes
Will always live within my heart.

LaVerne P. Larson

Photo Overleaf, SUNFLOWER FIELD, Gene Ahrens

Reflections of Peace

Peace is the whiteness of new-fallen snow,
Rain gently falling to the earth below,
The glorious setting of a golden sun,
A majestic sunrise that comes with dawn,
Deep, deep greenness of rolling hills,
Flowing rivers in the valley still.

Peace is the sweetness of a rose so rare,
Friends who comfort in times of despair,
Stars shining brightly in the heavens at night,
Beautiful lyrics in which lovers delight,
Waters serene upon the ceasing tide,
The unseen friend who walks beside.

Peace is the blueness of an infinite sky,
The carefree spirit of a butterfly,
Spring bursting forth in its cloak of yellow,
Rows of haystacks in an autumn meadow,
A rainbow trail that follows the storm,
Happiness in knowing the day's work is done.

Peace is the joy of a brand new day,
Faith to wave one's fears away,
Footprints stamped on timeless sand,
Unselfish service of a fellowman,
Blessed tears that cleanse the soul,
Memories reminiscent of days of old.

Peace is prayer in an hour sublime,
Strength renewed from a power divine,
Love that endures throughout the years,
Friendship eternal that time fulfills,
The substance that binds life's delicate threads,
The quality of existence where angels tread.

Jean Manning

A Nature Creed

I believe in the brook as it wanders
  from hillside into glade;

I believe in the breeze as it whispers
  when evening's shadows fade.

I believe in the roar of the river
  as it dashes from high cascade;

I believe in the cry of the tempest
  'mid the thunder's cannonade.

I believe in the light of shining stars;
I believe in the sun and the moon.

I believe in the flash of lightning;
I believe in the night-bird's croon.

I believe in the faith of the flowers;
I believe in the rock and sod,

For in all of these appeareth clear
  the handiwork of God.

Author Unknown

The Day Is Done

The day is done, and the darkness
   Falls from the wings of night,
As a feather is wafted downward
   From an eagle in his flight.

I see the lights of the village
   Gleam through the rain and the mist,
And a feeling of sadness comes o'er me
   That my soul cannot resist:

A feeling of sadness and longing,
   That is not akin to pain,
And resembles sorrow only
   As the mist resembles the rain.

Come, read to me some poem,
   Some simple and heartfelt lay,
That shall soothe this restless feeling,
   And banish the thoughts of day.

Not from the grand old masters,
   Not from the bards sublime,
Whose distant footsteps echo
   Through the corridors of time.

For, like strains of martial music,
    Their mighty thoughts suggest
Life's endless toil and endeavor;
    And tonight I long for rest.

Read from some humbler poet,
    Whose songs gushed from his heart,
As showers from the clouds of summer,
    Or tears from the eyelids start;

Who, through long days of labor,
    And nights devoid of ease,
Still heard in his soul the music
    Of wonderful melodies.

Such songs have power to quiet
    The restless pulse of care,
And come like the benediction
    That follows after prayer.

Then read from the treasured volume
    The poem of thy choice,
And lend to the rhyme of the poet
    The beauty of thy voice.

And the night shall be filled with music,
    And the cares, that infest the day,
Shall fold their tents, like the Arabs,
    And as silently steal away.

Henry Wadsworth Longfellow

Discover the Glory of Autumn in *ideals*

Clear blue skies; crisp, clean air; brilliant red and gold leaves—all these and more add to the beauty of the season. And you can share the joys of this time of year with friends by giving a subscription to *Ideals,* starting with our next issue, *Autumn Ideals.*

One of our friends, Mrs. Doris E. Johnson, of Worcester, Massachusetts, recently shared her thoughts about *Ideals* with us. She writes:

> *Each time I receive my* Ideals, *I think they have outdone themselves in this issue; but yesterday I received the* Easter *issue, which is absolutely the best.*
>
> *When I read your magazine, I feel at peace. The photography is excellent; whether it is the flowers or other scenes, they are great. The stories, poems...in other words, I like everything about the magazine.*

Thank you, Mrs. Johnson! We hope all our readers find such delight in the magazine and will let us know.

ACKNOWLEDGMENTS

FOR JOHN'S GIRL from the book *CRIPPLE CREEK DAYS* by Mabel Barbee Lee, Copyright © 1958 by Mabel Barbee Lee, published by Doubleday & Company, Inc.; FERN HILL from *SELECTED WRITINGS OF DYLAN THOMAS,* reprinted by permission of Harold Ober Associates, Incorporated, copyright 1946 by New Directions; NATURE'S CREED by Author Unknown from *MASTERPIECES OF RELIGIOUS VERSE,* James Dalton Morrison, ed., copyright © 1948 by Harper & Bros.; THE LAKE ISLE OF INNISFREE taken from *THE COLLECTED POEMS OF W. B. YEATS,* used by permission of A. P. Watt, Ltd., London, England on behalf of Anne Yeats and Michael B. Yeats. Our sincere thanks to the following whose addresses we were unable to locate: the estate of Anne Campbell for THE COUNTRY SCHOOL; Van Chandler for STREAK OF GOLD; Mildred Potts for THE BANDSTAND; Hazel Rugg for OUR HOMEMADE SWING.